COMETS, METEORS, AND ASTEROIDS

COMETS, METEORS, AND ASTEROIDS
ROCKS IN SPACE

by David J. Darling

Illustrated by Jeanette Swofford

DILLON PRESS, INC.   MINNEAPOLIS, MINNESOTA

The photographs are reproduced through the courtesy of the American Museum of Natural History, Hale Observatories, the Jet Propulsion Laboratory of the California Institute of Technology, John LaBorde, Dennis Milon, the National Aeronautics and Space Administration, and the U.S. Geological Survey.

Dillon Press, Inc., 242 Portland Avenue South
Minneapolis, Minnesota 55415

Printed in the United States of America

Library of Congress Cataloging in Publication Data

Darling, David J.
    Comets, meteors, and asteroids.

    Summary: Describes the origins,
characteristics, and behavior of comets, meteors,
and the largest of the space rocks, asteroids.
    1. Comets—Juvenile literature 2. Meteors—
Juvenile literature. 3. Planets, Minor—Juvenile
literature. 4. Geology—Juvenile literature.
[1. Comets. 2. Meteors. 3. Planets, Minor] 1. Title.
QB721.5.D37   1984   523.6   84-14275
ISBN 0-87518-264-X

5   6   7   8   9   10   91   90   89

✳ Contents

Comet, Meteor, and Asteroid Facts 6

*Questions and Answers about Comets, Meteors,
and Asteroids* 9

1 Beware, Low-Flying Space Rocks 13
2 Comets: The Fiery Snowballs 19
3 Meteor Showers and Shooting Stars 31
4 Asteroids: The Hurtling Mountains 39
5 Meteorites: Stones from the Sky 47

Appendix A: Discover for Yourself 53

*Appendix B: Amateur Astronomy Groups in the
United States, Canada, and Great
Britain* 55

Glossary 56

Suggested Reading 62

Index 63

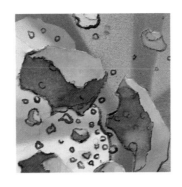

Comet, Meteor, and Asteroid Facts

Famous Comets

Name	First Seen	Period of Orbit (Year)
Halley's Comet	Before 240 B.C.	76-79
Tycho Brahe's Comet	1577	Unknown
Biela's Comet	1772	6.6-6.8
Encke's Comet	1786	3.3
Comet Flaugergues	1811	3,000
Comet Pons-Winnecke	1819	5.6-6.3
Great Comet of 1843	1843	513
Donati's Comet	1858	2,000
Great Comet of 1882	1882	760
Comet Morehouse	1908	Unknown
Comet Schwassmann-Wachmann I	1927	16.1-16.4
Comet Humason	1961	2,900
Comet Ikeya-Seki	1965	880
Comet Tago-Sato-Kosaka	1969	420,000
Comet Bennett	1969	1,680
Comet Kohoutek	1973	75,000
Comet West	1976	500,000

Important Meteor Showers

Shower	Best Date to Watch
Quadrantid	January 3
Lyrid	April 21
Eta Aquarid	May 4
Delta Aquarid	July 29
Perseid	August 12
Orionid	October 21
Taurid, North	November 4
Taurid, South	November 16
Leonid	November 17
Geminid	December 14

Largest Asteroids

Name	Distance Across (Diameter)
Ceres	623 miles (1,003 kilometers)
Pallas	378 miles (608 kilometers)
Vesta	334 miles (538 kilometers)
Hygeia	280 miles (450 kilometers)

 Questions & Answers about Comets, Meteors, and Asteroids

Q. Which was the first asteroid to be discovered?
A. Ceres, in 1801. It is also the largest asteroid.

Q. How much does Ceres weigh?
A. About 1,200,000,000,000,000,000,000 (one thousand, two hundred billion billion) tons. This makes it about 5,000 times lighter than the earth.

Q. Which is the smallest asteroid?
A. There are probably many asteroids, just a few hundred feet across, that we still don't know about. The smallest found so far is Hathor, a tiny world less than half a mile in diameter.

Q. In crossing the asteroid belt between Mars and Jupiter, could a spacecraft crash into an asteroid?
A. It's possible, but unlikely. The first four probes to enter the asteroid belt all made it through safely, and the asteroids appear to be far enough apart to make the chances of a crash quite small.

Q. Could an asteroid have killed the dinosaurs?
A. Some scientists think so. They believe that a small asteroid may have hit the earth about 65 million years ago. The material that it threw into the atmosphere may have blocked out the sun's heat and made the earth too cold for the dinosaurs to survive.

Q. Can any asteroid be seen without a telescope or binoculars?
A. Yes, the asteroid Vesta. It is just bright enough to be seen by someone with good eyesight who knows exactly where to look.

Q. Which comet had the longest tail?
A. In recorded times, the Great Comet of 1843. Its tail stretched out for 205 million miles (330 million kilometers), or more than twice the distance from the earth to the sun.

Q. Which comet has been seen the most times?
A. Encke's comet. It takes only 3.3 years to go around the sun and has been seen more than 50 times.

Q. What is the highest speed with which meteors enter our atmosphere?
A. About 45 miles per second (72 kilometers per second).

Q. What is the largest meteorite that ever fell on the United States?
A. The Willamette meteorite, weighing 14 tons, which fell in Oregon.

11

COMET WEST, PHOTOGRAPHED FROM SULLIVAN, NEW HAMPSHIRE, EARLY IN THE MORNING OF MARCH 7, 1976.

1 Beware, Low-Flying Space Rocks

On the morning of June 30, 1908, in a lonely Russian valley, there was a huge explosion. Tall trees were laid flat across a wide area, and the bang was felt hundreds of miles away. Whatever caused the explosion had come from outer space.

Could it have been an alien spaceship that had lost control while trying to land? Was it perhaps a tiny "black hole" that had come to earth from a distant part of the universe? In fact, neither of them caused this great explosion. The famous **Tunguska event,** * as it's called, was probably caused by a **comet** that burned up as it rushed through our atmosphere.

In 1937, a mountain-sized boulder called **Hermes** whizzed by the earth at a distance of just 500,000 miles (800,000 kilometers). As quickly as it came, it vanished again into the depths of space. More recently, in 1976, another large runaway rock, named **1976 UA,** approached to within 750,000 miles (1,200,000 kilometers) of our planet. Both Hermes and 1976 UA were visiting **asteroids.**

In almost any science museum, you'll find examples of smaller space rocks, called **meteorites,** that have crashed into the earth. But not all meteorites are small. If

*Words in **bold type** are explained in the glossary at the end of this book.

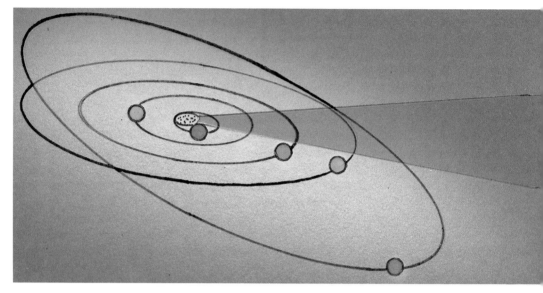

This drawing shows the planets in their orbits around the sun. On the right-hand page, the sun is the yellow ball at the center of the solar system. Moving around the sun are the planets Mercury, Venus, Earth, and Mars. The part of solar system shown

you travel to the northern Arizona desert, you may see the great **Barringer crater.** This three-quarter-mile-wide pit was made thousands of years ago by a giant meteorite. If you gaze into the sky on any clear night, you may see bright streaks of light, or **shooting stars.** These are caused by tiny **meteors** burning up as they plunge into the earth's atmosphere.

What could be more thrilling than these strange, often unexpected visitors? They bring with them matter that has journeyed for **trillions** of miles and that is **billions** of years old. They have traveled through regions that no human eye has ever seen. Yet the comets, asteroids, and meteors that crash into, or pass close by, the earth are just a few of the billions that wander through our vast neighborhood of space.

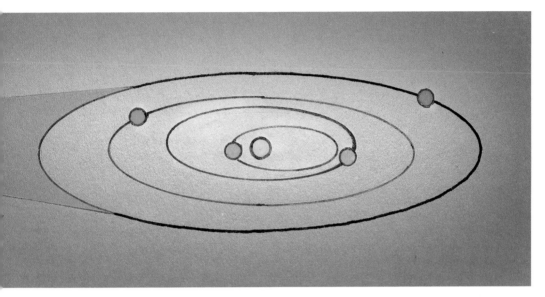

on the right is shown on the left-hand page by the small circle with the dots in it. The orbits of Jupiter, Saturn, Uranus, Neptune, and Pluto on the left are much farther from the sun than the orbits of the planets on the right.

The Kingdom of the Sun

The part of space in which we live is called the **solar system.** It contains the sun, an ordinary, yellow star, and all of the objects that go around it.

In terms of size and weight, the sun is the most important member of the solar system. Because of its great weight, it has a strong pull of **gravity.** And because of its strong pull of gravity, the sun forces everything else in its kingdom to move around it in huge curved paths called **orbits.**

Most important of the orbiting objects are the **planets.** There are nine, ranging in size from mighty Jupiter, at 88,700 miles (142,700 kilometers) in **diameter,** to tiny Pluto, at just 2,000 miles (3,200 kilometers).

Next come the **moons,** or **satellites,** of the planets.

15

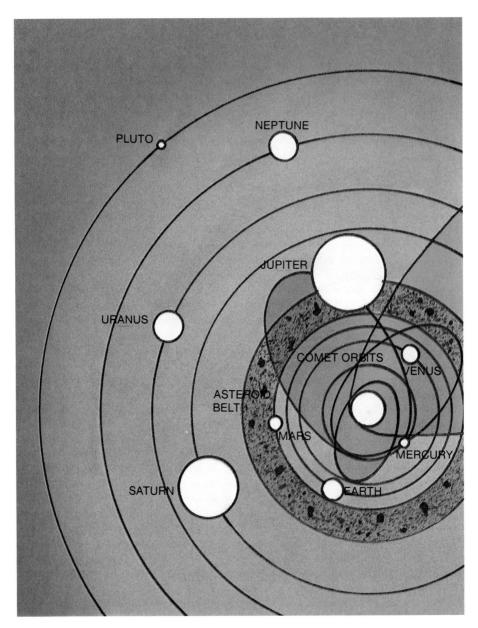

In this drawing of the solar system, the outside edges of the areas shaded in red show the orbits of several comets around the sun. The orange area between the orbits of Mars and Jupiter is the great asteroid belt.

Dust clouds from old comets orbit the sun along the paths once followed by the comets. These clouds cause meteor showers on earth.

Like our own moon, these objects orbit about their parent world. Biggest of these is Jupiter's Ganymede, at 3,278 miles (5,274 kilometers) in diameter. Smallest are the odd-shaped moons, such as Mars's Deimos, which is only 9 miles (14½ kilometers) across.

Finally, come the comets, meteors, and asteroids. They are small in size, ranging from an asteroid 623 miles (1,003 kilometers) in diameter to tiny meteors too small to be seen. But they are huge in number. Scientists already know of hundreds of comets, thousands of asteroids, and **millions** of meteors. Countless more are waiting to be discovered. In addition, there are now plans to send spacecraft to some of these small, wandering bodies to uncover the secrets that are locked within them.

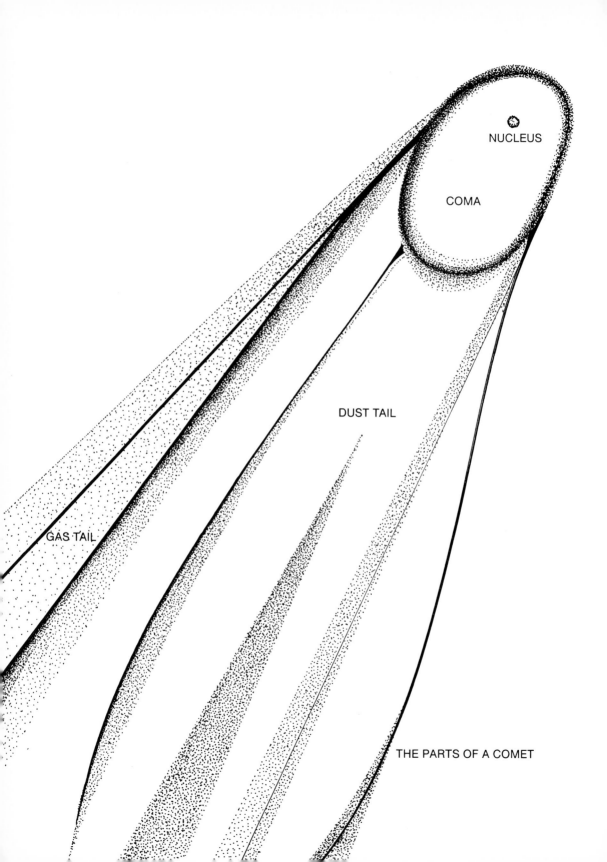

NUCLEUS

COMA

DUST TAIL

GAS TAIL

THE PARTS OF A COMET

2 Comets: The Fiery Snowballs

Nothing is quite as exciting as a really bright comet. It may be seen for weeks, even during the day. Like a rocket flame, its tail may stretch halfway across the sky.

But such a comet may come only once in a lifetime. Most, even at their brightest, can only be seen with a telescope. The few that can be seen with human eyes alone are usually just faint smudges or hazy streaks in the night sky.

Comets are among the most mysterious objects in the solar system. They appear from the darkest depths of the sun's kingdom. They hurtle by the inner planets, corner around the sun, and for a short time can be seen from the earth. Then they are gone, lost again in the blackness of space.

The Lonely Journey of a Comet

A comet has only a tiny solid part, called a **nucleus.** This part is no more than a few miles across. The nucleus probably looks like a dirty snowball—a chunk of ice and frozen gases in which there are bits of rock and dust. Right at its center, there may be a small, rocky **core.**

A comet, like a planet, goes around the sun. But a comet's orbit is long and flattened, different from that of a

Comet Ikeya-Seki, photographed by the U.S. Naval Observatory on April 3, 1978.

planet. It carries the comet quite close to the sun at one end, and very far away at the other.

For many years, a comet will travel on the part of its orbit that lies far from the sun. It may journey for hundreds or thousands of years in the outer solar system. Sometimes it goes beyond the orbit of the most distant planet, Pluto. During this time, since it gets very little warmth from the sun, it remains just a small ball of ice and rock in space. Because it gives off no light of its own, it cannot be seen, even through big telescopes, from earth.

At last, its path begins to carry it towards the inner solar system again. It passes, in turn, the orbits of Pluto, and of the giant planets: Neptune, Uranus, Saturn, and Jupiter. Gradually, the sun's heat starts to release some of

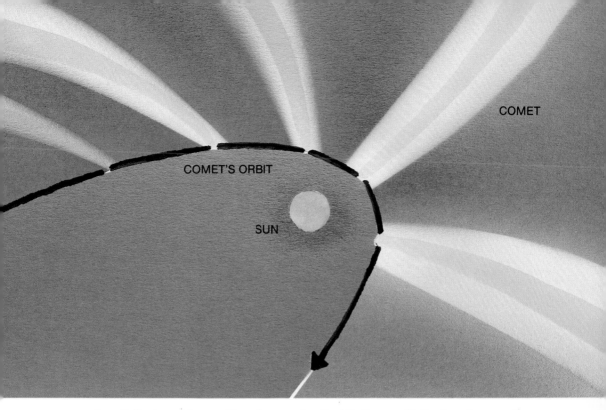

COMET

COMET'S ORBIT

SUN

An artist's view of the position of a comet as it orbits the sun. Notice how the comet's tail always points away from the sun.

the gases from the surface of the comet's frozen nucleus. These gases form a fuzzy, glowing ball, called the **coma,** around the nucleus.

The coma grows as the comet plunges in towards the sun. Soon, it can be seen through telescopes on earth. It may grow until it's more than 100,000 miles (160,000 kilometers) across—about half the distance from the earth to the moon.

At the same time, the comet may begin to grow a **tail.** This bright part is made of glowing matter that has been blown out of the coma by the **solar wind**—a stream of particles that flows outwards from the sun. The tail can stretch out for millions of miles. Because it's blown by the solar wind, it always points *away* from the sun as the comet moves around its orbit.

21

Arend-Roland comet, photographed on April 27, 1957, at Mount Wilson Observatory. See if you can spot the parts of this comet.

Comet Cunningham, photographed December 21, 1940. The shape of this comet's coma and tail is different than that of the Arend-Roland comet.

Comets may have a gas tail—one that's narrow, straight, and pointed exactly away from the sun. Or, they may have a dust tail—one that's wider and more curved. Many comets have both a gas and a dust tail, along with such markings as streaks, spirals, and rays. Some have no tail at all, just a fuzzy, round coma.

The Life and Death of a Comet

The biggest difference among comets is in the way they move around the sun. First, there are **long-period comets.** These travel around huge, stretched-out orbits that carry them much farther from the sun than any planet. Long-period comets may take thousands of years just to make one trip around the sun.

Then, there are **short-period comets.** These have

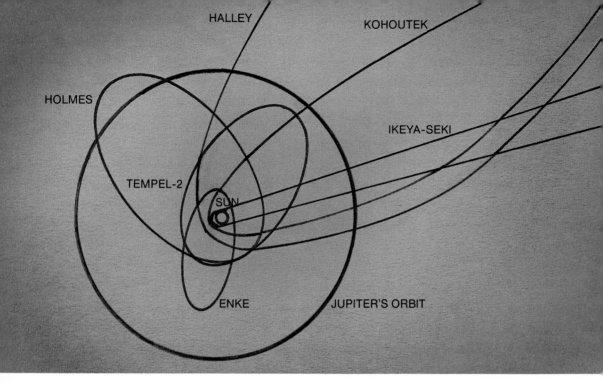

HALLEY

KOHOUTEK

HOLMES

IKEYA-SEKI

TEMPEL-2

SUN

ENKE

JUPITER'S ORBIT

This drawing shows the orbits of some well-known comets in relation to the sun and Jupiter's orbit. The short-period comets stay within the solar system, while the long-period comets travel vast distances and may take thousands of years to complete one orbit.

smaller orbits that extend only as far as the outer planets. They make their round-the-sun trips in less than a hundred years.

Where do these two different kinds of comets come from? Some scientists believe there is a huge cloud of dark, frozen comets, called the **Oort Cloud,** that moves around the sun at a very great distance. It's probably 50,000 times farther from the sun than the earth is and may contain as many as 100 billion comets.

Once in a while, the gravity of a distant star may change the path of a comet in the Oort Cloud and make it plunge inwards towards the sun. The comet will still take a very long time to go around its new orbit. Now, though, we'll be able to see it as it comes close to the sun. It will be a long-period comet.

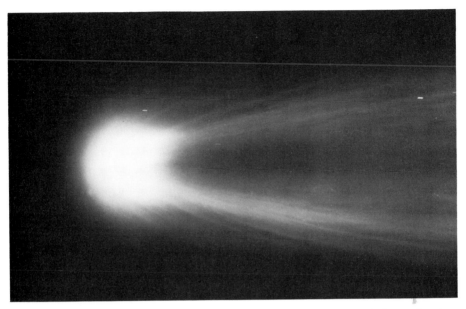

Halley's comet, photographed on May 8, 1910. Halley's is a short-period comet and a member of the Neptune family.

If the comet happens to pass close to a large planet, it may have its orbit changed again. Instead of a long-period comet, it may become a short-period one. Then its new path lies much closer to the sun.

Most of the short-period comets—about 60 in all—belong to the **Jupiter family.** Jupiter's powerful gravity has forced them into quite small orbits that take them only about 500 million miles (800 million kilometers) from the sun.

The brightest and best known of the short-period comets is **Halley's comet.** Halley's is a member of the **Neptune family.** At its farthest, it is more than 3 billion miles away and much too dim to be seen. Every 76 years, though, it swings close by the sun. As it speeds around the sun, it gives us a wonderful view of its brilliant coma

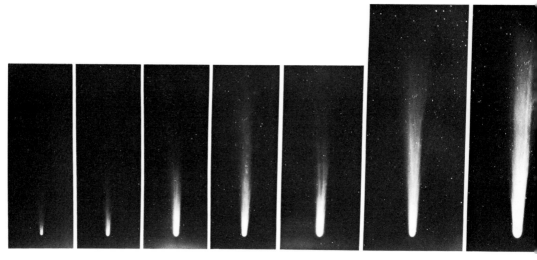

Seven views of Halley's comet between April 26 and May 6, 1910.

and its gleaming, 100-million-mile-long tail.

Halley's comet will visit us again in 1986. We should be able to see it quite clearly from earth. And, even more exciting, several spacecraft will be launched to study it from close up in space. For the first time, we might catch a glimpse of the tiny, mysterious heart of a comet—the nucleus.

At its closest, Halley's comet comes to within 50 million miles (80 million kilometers) of the sun—well within the earth's orbit. Most comets stay farther away from the sun. A few, however, come even closer.

Some comets, called **sun-grazers,** may crash straight into the sun, or get so close that they burn up. Once in a while, a sun-grazer will hold together as it speeds around the sun. Then the sun's strong force of gravity may hurl it

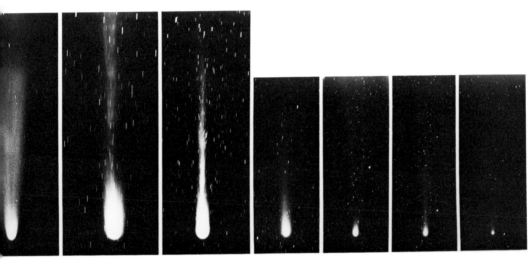

Seven more views of Halley's comet between May 7 and June 11, 1910.

into a new path that carries it out of the solar system forever.

A comet has quite a short life compared to that of most objects in space. Each time it comes close to the sun, its nucleus shrinks a little more. The supply of ice and dust needed to make the glowing coma and tail grows less and less and finally runs out.

A long-period comet may last for millions of years. A short-period one, though, may wear out after just a few thousand years.

What happens to a comet as it starts to get old? If it's like **Encke's comet,** with a rocky core in the middle of its nucleus, it may gradually fade away.

Encke's comet has the shortest orbit of any comet. It speeds around the sun once every 3.3 years. Encke's has

In this picture, an artist shows how Biela's comet may have looked as its nucleus split

no tail and only a very small coma. It seems to have lost most of the dusty, icy mixture needed to make a tail and is fast becoming just a dark, wandering boulder.

If a comet is like **Biela's comet,** though, it may break up in a much more exciting way. Biela's comet was discovered in 1832. Like Encke's comet, it was a member of the Jupiter family. Biela's was a short-period comet going around the sun once every 6.7 years.

On its return in 1839, it was lost in the sun's glare and couldn't be seen from earth. When it came back again in 1846, however, scientists were able to study it closely. They were amazed at what they saw. Biela's comet had split into two pieces! When the comet was next seen, in 1852, the pieces had moved 1½ million miles apart. What had happened to cause it to break up?

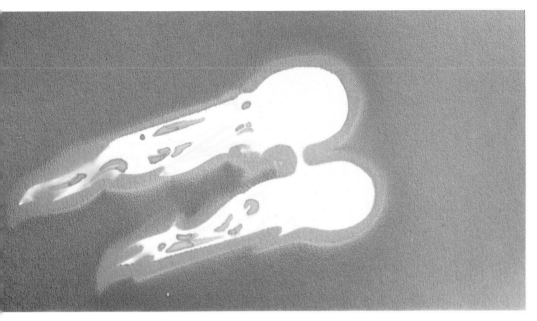

apart between its approach to the sun in 1839 and 1846.

Biela's comet, it seems, was nothing more than a crumbly mixture of ice and dust. It had no rocky center at all. On its approach to the sun in 1839, it must have become so heated that its nucleus simply broke apart.

That breakup, though, was not quite the end of Biela's comet. It's true that the comet, itself, had gone forever. After 1852, it was never seen again. But old Biela had a ghost, and, like those of many other comets, it still comes back to haunt us each year.

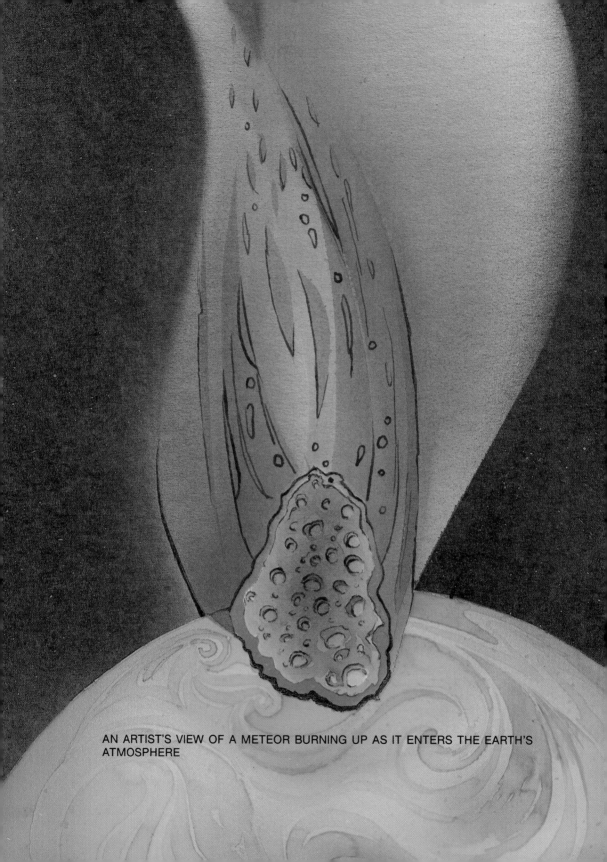

AN ARTIST'S VIEW OF A METEOR BURNING UP AS IT ENTERS THE EARTH'S ATMOSPHERE

3 Meteor Showers and Shooting Stars

Except for aircraft and satellites launched by humans from earth, most objects in the night sky hardly appear to move at all. Even comets seem to crawl along at a snail's pace, barely changing position from one hour to the next.

But there's one kind of space object that flashes across the night sky faster than the eye can follow. For a second or two it blazes a thin white trail—and then it is gone. This object is a meteor or shooting star.

A meteor is a tiny piece of rock or dust that burns up as it speeds through the earth's atmosphere. Far from being star-size, it may be no bigger than a grain of sand. It enters our atmosphere at a speed as high as 150,000 miles per hour. It is heated and begins to glow about 100 miles above the ground. Glowing white-hot, it lasts for a few more seconds while it plunges to a height of around 50 miles. Then it is burned up and its remains drift in the air as the tiniest of dust fragments.

On any clear night, you should be able to spot as many as 10 meteors an hour flashing across the sky. Just gaze upwards and be patient! The meteors that you see will be just a few of the 20 million or so that burn up in our atmosphere every day.

In fact, the meteors that bump into the earth are just

A meteor flashes through the night sky on August 12, 1980, as photographed from Harvard, Massachusetts.

a few of the billions of **meteoroids** that go around the sun. *Meteoroid* is the name given by scientists to any kind of small particle in space. A meteoroid becomes a *meteor* only when it enters the earth's atmosphere.

Meteoroids come in sizes ranging from tiny grains too small to be seen—**micrometeoroids**—to chunks roughly the size of a grape. They form a great cloud, called the **zodiacal cloud,** that surrounds the sun and through which the planets move. The zodiacal cloud probably weighs as much as 10 trillion tons.

Most of the meteoroids in the zodiacal cloud have come from comets. These bits and pieces were once stuck in the nuclei of comets and they were shot out in their tails. After thousands or millions of years, the meteoroids drifted into a huge cloud. The zodiacal cloud is really nothing more than a graveyard for comets that broke up long ago.

But what about comets that are still alive, or that have died only recently? Their dust hasn't had time to drift into the zodiacal cloud. Where is it?

Here's where we return to find the ghost of Biela's comet. Remember that the comet, itself, was never seen again after its return to the sun, in two widely separated pieces, in 1852. But in 1872, the earth passed through a tremendous **meteor storm** at just the place where scientists would have expected to find the old comet. What had happened?

Biela's comet had completely broken up, setting free all the particles that had once formed its "dusty snowball" nucleus. Those particles were still clumped together

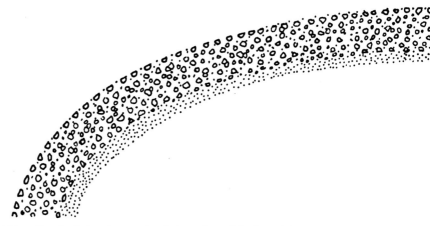

This drawing shows the dust cloud spread out along the orbit of an old comet. When

around where the old comet had been. They were still moving around its old orbit. But now, they were separate meteoroids. In 1872, a large number of them smashed into the earth's atmosphere and caused the **Bieliid** meteor storm.

A meteor storm happens only rarely, when the earth passes through a part of a comet's orbit where there is a lot of dust. The storm might come from the remains of a broken nucleus, as in the case of the Bieliids. It could also be caused by a small piece of the comet that split off from the main part.

Meteor showers are much more common than storms. A number of them take place every year and, again, they are all known to be connected with comets.

As comets get older, dust from them gradually

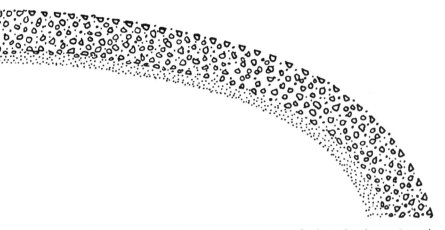

the earth passes through part of a comet's dust cloud, a meteor shower happens.

spreads out along their orbits. Dust from Encke's comet, for example, now completely litters the path of the old, worn-out nucleus. Meteor showers happen when the earth, on its yearly trip around the sun, passes close by these comet orbits and sweeps up some of the dust they contain.

The **Leonids,** for instance, are meteors from the comet **Temple-Tuttle.** They happen every year around November 17. The **Perseids** are from the comet **Swift-Tuttle** and can be seen between the end of July and the middle of August.

Weaker showers include the **Taurids,** from Encke's comet, and the Bieliids, or **Andromedids,** from Biela's comet. In each case, the meteor shower is named after the group of stars, or **constellation,** in the part of the sky

The Leonid meteor shower on November 17, 1966, turned into a rare meteor storm. This photograph was made just after dawn from Kitt Peak, Arizona. The meteors are the long, bright streaks of light.

from which it seems to come.

Sometimes, one of the famous yearly showers will turn into a storm. Such a storm happened last just after dawn on November 17, 1966, over the western United States. Meteors from the Leonid shower started falling at the rate of 40 a second—or 144,000 an hour! Normally, the heaviest shower is the Perseids with about 70 meteors an hour. Those who were lucky enough to see the 1966 Leonids witnessed one of the heaviest meteor storms on record.

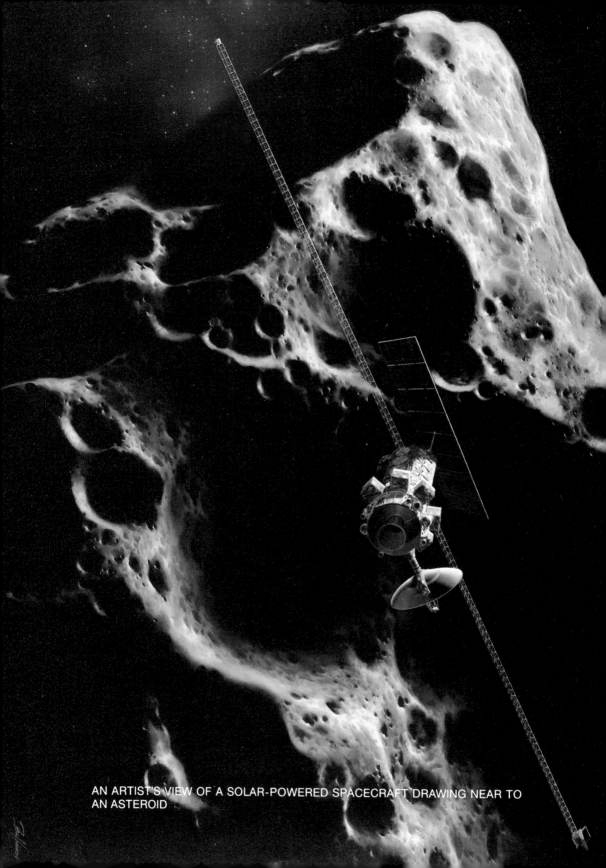

AN ARTIST'S VIEW OF A SOLAR-POWERED SPACECRAFT DRAWING NEAR TO AN ASTEROID

4 Asteroids: The Hurtling Mountains

By far the largest of space rocks are the asteroids. Most of them lie in a great belt—the **asteroid belt**—that goes around the sun between the orbits of Mars and Jupiter.

Scientists used to think that the asteroids were the pieces of a planet that broke up long ago. But today, we know that they could never have formed a planet-sized world. Even if all the asteroids were gathered together, they would weigh only about one-twentieth as much as the moon.

Many of the 2,500 known asteroids would fit easily within the limits of a small city. Some would span only a few city blocks. Yet, others are much larger.

The largest of the asteroids is **Ceres,** which is 623 miles (1,003 kilometers) in diameter. It weighs as much as all the other asteroids combined, and is bigger than many satellites. Its nearest rivals are **Pallas** at 378 miles (608 kilometers) in diameter, **Vesta** at 334 miles (538 kilometers), and **Hygeia** at 280 miles (450 kilometers).

Only Ceres and Pallas appear to be roughly round, like a planet. Most asteroids have an odd shape.

They have different makeups, too. Asteroids nearer the sun, in the inner part of the asteroid belt, tend to be made of heavy rock or metal. They are called **S-type** (S for

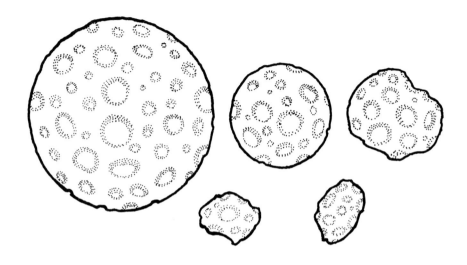

Among the asteroids, only Ceres and Pallas are roughly round in shape. This drawing shows Ceres, Pallas, and some other odd-shaped asteroids.

silicate, a heavy kind of rock) or **M-type** (*M* for *metal*).

Asteroids farther from the sun, in the middle and outer parts of the belt, tend to be made of lighter rock and ice. They are called **C-type** (*C* for *carbonaceous,* a lighter kind of rock). How do scientists explain these differences?

Billions of years ago, there were probably far fewer asteroids than there are today. Perhaps only about one hundred moved around the sun between Mars and Jupiter. These were the "original" asteroids—objects that formed at the same time as the planets.

The asteroids that formed closer to the sun were made, like the inner planets, of heavier substances. Those that formed farther away were made, like the giant, outer worlds, of lighter substances.

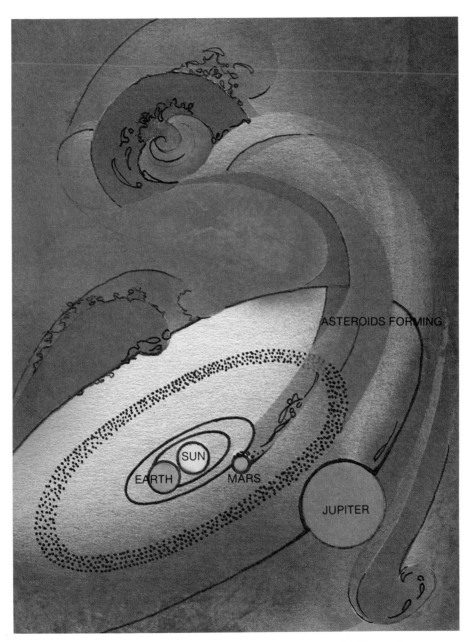

An artist's view of how the original asteroids may have formed billions of years ago when the solar system was taking shape.

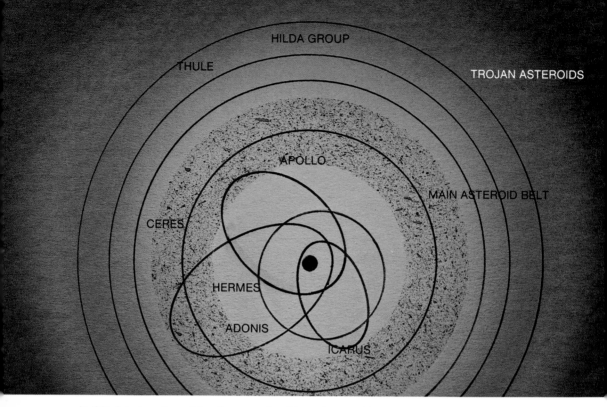

In this drawing, the orbits of some asteroids and asteroid groups are shown in relation to the sun, at the center of the picture.

Crashes among the original asteroids gradually broke them up into smaller pieces. Those in the inner part of the belt formed today's M-type and S-type asteroids. Those in the outer part became the C-types. Only Ceres, and perhaps Pallas, have stayed in about the same form as they were long ago.

Some asteroids have wandered away from the main belt to follow new paths around the sun. The **Trojan asteroids**, for example, share the same orbit as Jupiter. They form two little groups—one ahead of the giant planet, the other behind it. These groups are exactly at the points where the gravity of Jupiter and the sun pull with equal strength.

Strangely enough, the biggest of the Trojans, **Hektor,** may actually be two objects. The two parts may be stuck

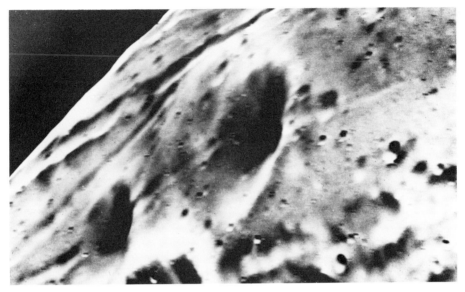

In 1977 *Viking I* took this close-up photograph of the Martian moon, Phobos, from just 75 miles (120 kilometers) away. Phobos may be an old asteroid that was captured by Mars's gravity.

together or circling closely about each other. Together with Pallas, and the smaller **Victoria,** it's one of the growing number of asteroids suspected of having a moon!

Asteroids may become moons, themselves, if they drift too close to a planet. Several of the outer satellites of Jupiter, and the outermost one of Saturn, are asteroids captured by the planets' strong pull of gravity. Both of Mars's moons, **Phobos** and **Deimos,** appear to be old asteroids, too.

Other asteroids—the so-called **Apollo objects**—follow paths that bring them closer to the sun than the earth. From time to time, one will have a close encounter with our world. In 1937, for example, tiny **Hermes** brushed by the earth at a distance of only 485,000 miles.

Apollo objects have orbits very much like those of

short-period comets. Could they, in fact, be the rocky cores of dead comets?

In 1983, scientists found an Apollo object, **1983 TB,** that skims by the sun at a distance of only 13 million miles (21 million kilometers) every 1½ years. More importantly, it follows exactly the same orbit as the **Geminid** meteor shower. This fact suggests that 1983 TB was once the comet that broke up and formed the Geminids. If it is, then perhaps all of the fifty or so Apollo objects are really dead comets.

Another mystery object that seems part comet, part asteroid, is **Chiron.** Discovered in 1977, it circles the sun farther out than any known asteroid—between the orbits of Saturn and Uranus.

At about 250 miles (400 kilometers) in diameter, Chi-

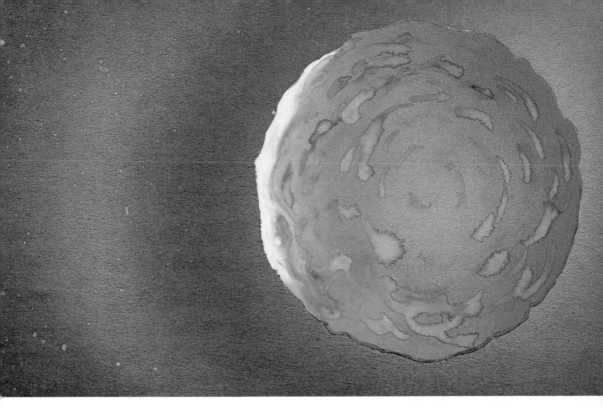

An artist's view of Chiron, which circles the sun between the orbits of Saturn and Uranus. Chiron could be a large, frozen comet that has swung into a strange orbit.

ron seems too big to be a comet. But, if it's an asteroid, what is it doing so far from the sun? Some scientists think that Chiron may be a large frozen comet, fresh from the Oort Cloud, that has swung into a strange orbit. Others believe that it may be just the first in a new belt of asteroids that lies beyond Saturn.

BARRINGER CRATER, NEAR WINSLOW, ARIZONA, WAS MADE BY A LARGE ME-
TEORITE THAT CRASHED INTO THE EARTH LONG AGO.

5 Meteorites: Stones From the Sky

The biggest space rocks, comets and asteroids, hardly ever hit the earth. The smallest, meteors, burn up in the atmosphere. But medium-sized space rocks quite often crash into the earth's surface. These are called meteorites.

About 500 meteorites smash into the earth every year. Since most fall in out-of-the-way places, or into the sea, they are difficult to find and to study. But a few are found. These are looked at carefully to discover what they are made of and where, in space, they may have come from. To scientists, they are very important. Apart from rocks brought back from the moon, they are the only samples we have of matter from beyond our planet.

Meteorites can range in size from small pebbles to huge boulders. The largest ever found weighs 60 tons, measures 10 feet across, and landed thousands of years ago in Namibia (South-West Africa). It has never been moved from where it fell. Another, discovered in Greenland, weighs about 34 tons. It is now on display in the American Museum of Natural History in New York.

Even larger meteorites have hit the earth in the past. They have left behind huge **impact craters**—hollows in the ground surrounded by steep, rounded walls.

The Willamette meteorite weighs more than 15 tons and is the largest meteorite ever found in the United States. It is now on display in the American Museum of Natural History.

The most famous crater, thought to be about 50,000 years old, is near Winslow, Arizona. Called the Barringer crater, it measures 4,000 feet across and was probably caused by a giant meteorite weighing around one million tons.

Older, more weathered craters, called **astroblemes,** have been found in remote parts of Canada, the Soviet Union, and South Africa. The most striking one of all is the **Vredefort Ring** in the Transvaal of South Africa. Measuring 30 miles across, it is the giant scar left by a mile-wide object that smashed into the earth about 250 million years ago.

Such big crashes are rare. But there have been one or two recent "near misses." In 1908, a large space rock exploded over the Tunguska River valley in Siberia.

Scientists now think that it was probably not a meteorite. Instead, they believe, this rock was a small comet that burned up as it raced through the atmosphere.

In 1972, a 1000-ton meteoroid streaked across the skies of the western United States. It flew safely by at a distance of just 36 miles (58 kilometers) above the earth before disappearing back into space.

Even when meteorites do hit the earth, they usually land far away from people. A few, though, have paid unexpected visits. On April 25, 1969, a one-pound space rock ended its journey by dropping through the roof of the Sprucefield police storehouse in Northern Ireland!

Meteorites are the best understood of all space rocks. They come in three main types: **stones, stony-irons,** and **irons.** Of these, stones are the most common. Only about

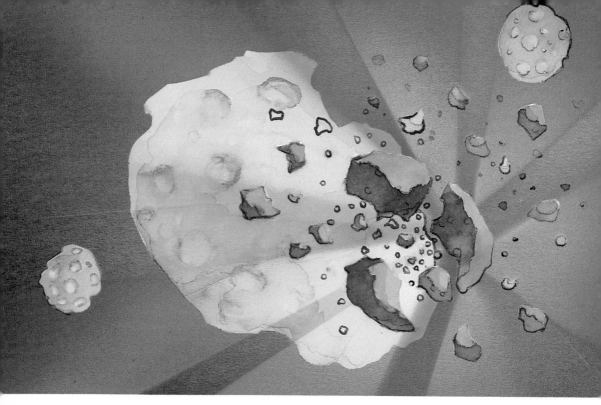

In this picture, an artist shows how asteroids crashing into each other in the past may have created meteorites that later found their way to the earth.

one in twenty meteorites is an iron, which is made of an iron-**nickel** mixture. Rarest of all are the stony-irons.

Some of the stones, called **chondrites,** are among the oldest objects ever found. Their age may be more than 4½ billion years—greater than that of the planets. To scientists, chondrites are exciting because they have been found to contain **organic matter.** This discovery proves that at least some of the substances on which life is based have also been formed in space.

No one is really sure where all of the 2,000 known meteorites have come from. It seems likely that many of them are pieces of asteroids that have broken off and found their way to earth. But the link between meteorites and asteroids isn't as strong as that between meteor showers and comets.

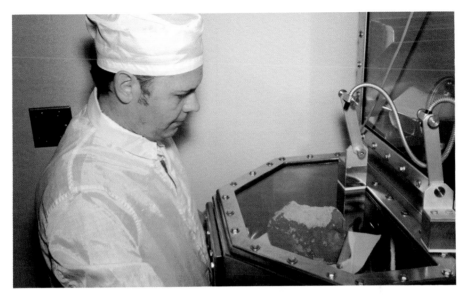

A scientist in the Johnson Space Center studies a meteorite from Antarctica. This meteorite has the same makeup as the surface of Mars as measured by the Viking spacecraft.

Perhaps new clues to help solve this mystery will come from Antarctica. For here, in the ice of the great southern continent, scientists have uncovered a vast number of frozen meteorites. The cold, dry climate has kept them exactly the way they were when they fell.

Already, an Antarctic meteorite has been found that may have come, not from an asteroid, but from the planet Mars! Scientists have compared the makeup of this unusual space rock with that of the Martian surface as measured by the Viking spacecraft. When they did, they found a near perfect match. It's possible that the rock was hurled into space, towards the earth, by another meteorite that crashed into Mars millions of years ago.

There are still many unanswered questions about the rocks that speed through space and sometimes come

This *Viking I* photo of the Martian surface shows craters that may have been made by meteorites. It is possible that such a meteorite knocked loose a chunk of Martian rock that was later found on earth in Antarctica.

close to our world. The mysteries of comets, asteroids, and meteors will be solved only when our spacecraft are sent to explore them.

In early 1986, that exploration will begin when five spacecraft fly out to meet Halley's comet. In the years that follow, it will continue. Spacecraft may chase other comets around the sun, fly through the heart of meteor storms, and land on the surface of the distant asteroids. All these missions will add to our understanding of the rocks in space.

Appendix A:
Discover For Yourself

1. *Spot a Meteor*

You can see meteors, or shooting stars, on any clear night of the year. It's best to look for them when you are away from bright city lights. Simply stare upwards for a few minutes, and you should see the thin white trail of a meteor flash across the sky. If you're patient, you may spot as many as 10 meteors in an hour.

On certain nights of the year, there are meteor showers. Each one is named after the constellation of stars from which it seems to come.

Try to spot the meteor showers listed below. To get help in locating them, visit your local planetarium, or refer to the meteors section in the *Yearbook of Astronomy*.

Shower	Dates	Best Night
Quadrantid	Jan. 1—Jan. 6	Jan. 3
Perseid	Jul. 25—Aug. 18	Aug. 12
Orionid	Oct. 16—Oct. 26	Oct. 21
Taurid	Oct. 20—Nov. 25	Nov. 4
Geminid	Dec. 7—Dec. 15	Dec. 14

2. Draw the Path of a Comet

Comets move in very long, stretched out orbits around the sun. The shape of these paths is an oval, or **ellipse**.

To draw an ellipse, begin by taping a big sheet of drawing paper onto a flat wooden board. Press two thumbtacks, three inches apart, halfway into the board and paper. Cut a piece of strong thread about a foot long and tie together its ends.

Next, loop the thread around the pins and stretch it tight with a pencil. Keep the pencil upright, the thread tight, and move the pencil around the whole loop. The shape you'll have drawn is an ellipse.

Try changing the distance between the pins. Try smaller distances—one or two inches— and larger distances—four or five inches. What do you notice? Which look more like the almost circular paths of planets? Which look like the long, narrow paths of comets?

Appendix B:
Amateur Astronomy Groups
in the United States,
Canada, and Great Britain

For information or resource materials about the subjects covered in this book, contact your local astronomy group, science museum, or planetarium. You may also write to one of the national amateur astronomy groups listed below.

United States
The Astronomical League
Donald Archer,
   Executive Secretary
P.O. Box 12821
Tucson, Arizona 85732

American Association of
   Variable Star Astronomers
187 Concord Avenue
Cambridge, Massachusetts 02138

Canada
The Royal Astronomical Society of Canada
La Société Royale d'Astronomie du Canada
Rosemary Freeman, Executive Secretary
136 Dupont Street
Toronto, Ontario M5R 1V2

Great Britain
Junior Astronomical Society
58 Vaughan Gardens
Ilford
Essex IG1 3PD England

British Astronomical Assoc.
Burlington House
Piccadilly
London W1V 0NL England

Glossary

Andromedids—a weak meteor shower that appears each year around November 25. It is the remains of Biela's comet and, for that reason, is also called the Bieliids

Apollo object—a kind of asteroid—about 50 of which are known—whose orbit carries it quite close to the sun. Apollo objects may be the rocky cores of dead comets

asteroid—the largest kind of space rock, measuring from a few hundred yards to a few hundred miles across. Most are found within the asteroid belt, though a few travel in other paths around the solar system

asteroid belt—the broad belt, stretching around the sun between the orbits of Mars and Jupiter, that contains most of the asteroids. It starts about 200 million miles (320 million kilometers) from the sun, and goes out to a distance of about 370 million miles (600 million kilometers)

astrobleme—a very old crater in the earth's surface, worn down by weather, that was made by a giant meteorite

Barringer crater—the most famous meteorite crater. Located in the northern Arizona desert, it is about three-quarters of a mile across. The crater was formed about 50,000 years ago by an object weighing roughly one million tons

Biela's comet—one of the most interesting comets ever seen. It broke into two pieces in 1845 and disappeared altogether a few years later. In its place was the Andromedid (Bieliid) meteor shower

Bieliids—see *Andromedids* and *Biela's comet*

billion—a thousand million. Written as 1,000,000,000

C-type asteroid—a kind of asteroid made up mainly of light rocks. C-type asteroids are found in the outer parts of the asteroid belt

Ceres—the largest asteroid known. It is 623 miles (1,003 kilometers) in diameter

Chiron—an object about 250 miles (450 kilometers) in diameter whose orbit lies between those of Saturn and Uranus. It may be a new kind of asteroid or a large frozen comet

chondrite—a kind of stone meteorite that has changed very little since it was formed as long as 4½ billion years ago

coma—the large ball of glowing gases and dust that surrounds a comet's nucleus when it is close to the sun

comet—an object made of frozen gases, dust, and pieces of rock, that moves around the sun in a very long, narrow orbit. The main part of a comet, the nucleus, is no more than a few miles in diameter

constellation—a pattern of stars in the sky. Examples are Orion,

Taurus, and Gemini

core—the small, heavy, central part of an object such as a planet, moon, asteroid, or comet

crater—a round, bowl-shaped hole made in the surface of a world by a meteorite or a volcano. See *impact crater*

Deimos—the smaller of the two moons of Mars. It measures 9 miles by 7½ miles and is thought to be a captured asteroid

diameter—the length of a straight line that runs from one side of an object to the other, passing through its center

ellipse—a long, oval shape. Comets move in long, stretched-out orbits around the sun. The orbits' shape is an ellipse

Encke's comet—the comet with the smallest orbit. It takes only 3.3 years to go around the sun

Geminids—a meteor shower that can be seen in

the first part of December.
It shares the same orbit as
the Apollo object, 1983 TB
gravity—the force by
which all objects pull on all
other objects. Gravity is
what makes the planets,
asteroids, and comets go
around the sun

Halley's comet—the
brightest and best known of
the short-period comets. It
takes 76 years to go around
the sun and will appear
next in January 1986
Hektor—the largest of the
Trojan asteroids, at 180
miles (290 kilometers) by
90 miles (145 kilometers). It
appears to be made of two
asteroids, either stuck
together or circling around
each other
Hermes—an Apollo asteroid whose orbit can carry it
very close to the earth
Hygeia—the fourth largest
asteroid known, at about
280 miles (450 kilometers)
in diameter

impact crater—the kind of
crater made by a falling

object such as a meteorite
iron—a kind of meteorite
made up of about
nine-tenths iron and
one-tenth nickel. It is also
the name of the most used
metal on earth

Jupiter family—a group of
about 60 short-period
comets whose orbits go out
only about as far as the
orbit of Jupiter

Leonids—a meteor shower,
caused by dust from the
comet Temple-Tuttle, which
takes place around
November 17
long-period comet—a
comet whose orbit goes out
far beyond the most distant
planet, Pluto. Long-period
comets may take thou-
sands, or even millions, of
years to go around the sun

M-type asteroid—a kind
of asteroid containing the
metals iron and nickel.
M-type asteroids are found
in the inner parts of the
asteroid belt
meteor—a small piece of

rock or dust that burns up as it passes through the earth's atmosphere

meteorite—a rock from space that reaches the earth's surface. Its weight may range from a few pounds to more than a million tons

meteoroid—the name given to any kind of small rock or piece of dust in space. A meteoroid becomes a *meteor* if it enters the earth's atmosphere, and a *meteorite* if it reaches the earth's surface

meteor shower—a rain of meteors that is seen when the earth crosses the dusty path of a comet

meteor storm—a very heavy rain of meteors that happens when the earth passes through an unusually dusty part of a comet's orbit

micrometeoroid—a tiny meteoroid, too small to be seen

million—a thousand thousand. Written as 1,000,000

moon—a natural object that circles around a planet or, possibly, an asteroid

Neptune family—a small group of short-period comets that includes the famous Halley's comet. Their orbits extend out about as far as the orbit of Neptune

nickel—a type of metal, found together with iron in some meteorites, asteroids, and the cores of planets

nucleus—the small, hard part of a comet. It is made of frozen gases in which there are bits of rock and dust. The nucleus is usually between one and ten miles in diameter

Oort Cloud—the giant cloud of frozen comets that is thought to circle the sun at a distance of more than a trillion miles

orbit—the curved path in which one object moves around another because of gravity. The paths that planets, comets, and asteroids follow around the sun, for example, are orbits

organic matter—any substance that is based on carbon. Organic matter is what living things are made of

Pallas—the second largest asteroid known, at 378 miles (608 kilometers) in diameter

Perseids—the biggest of the yearly meteor showers, caused by meteors from the comet Swift-Tuttle. They take place between the end of July and the middle of August

Phobos—the larger of the two moons of Mars, measuring 16½ miles (27 kilometers) by 13½ miles (22 kilometers). Like Deimos, it is thought to be a captured asteroid

planet—a rocky or icy world, at least several thousand miles in diameter, that orbits a star. The sun has nine planets

S-type asteroid—a kind of asteroid made mainly of heavy rock. S-type asteroids are found in the inner parts of the asteroid belt

satellite—see *moon*

shooting star—another name for meteor

short-period comet—a kind of comet whose orbit goes out only about as far as one of the giant planets. Most of the short-period comets are in the Jupiter family and take only a few years to go around the sun

solar system—the name given to the sun and everything that goes around it, including: planets, moons, asteroids, comets, and meteors

solar wind—the stream of tiny, fast-moving particles that is always blowing outwards from the surface of the sun

stone—the most common type of meteorite. It contains a mixture of different kinds of rock and crystals

stony-iron—a rare kind of meteorite, containing rocks together with the metals iron and nickel

sun-grazer—a type of comet that crashes into, or passes very close to, the sun

Swift-Tuttle—the comet that causes the Perseid

meteor shower

tail—the glowing stream of gas and dust that may stretch out for millions of miles behind a comet when it is close to the sun

Taurids—the weak meteor shower that happens every year between about October 20 and November 30. It is caused by dust from Encke's comet

Temple-Tuttle—the comet that causes the Leonid meteor shower

trillion—a thousand billion. Written as 1,000,000,000,000

Trojan asteroids—two groups of asteroids that move around the same orbit as Jupiter. They are always placed so that the pull of gravity on them from Jupiter and the sun is equal

Tunguska event—the name given to the great explosion that took place over and around the Tunguska River valley, Siberia, in 1908. It was probably caused by the nucleus of a small comet that blew up in the atmosphere

Vesta—the third largest asteroid known, at 334 miles (538 kilometers) in diameter

Victoria—a small asteroid, 75 miles (120 kilometers) in diameter, that is thought to have a tiny moon

Vredefort Ring—a huge crater in South Africa, measuring 30 miles across. It was probably made about 250 million years ago by a one-mile-wide meteorite

zodiacal cloud—the great cloud surrounding the sun that contains the dust of long-dead comets

1976 UA—a small Trojan asteroid that came within 750,000 miles of the earth in 1976

1983 TB—the Trojan asteroid whose orbit lies closest to the sun. It is believed to be the rocky core of a comet that broke up and formed the Geminid meteor shower

☀ Suggested Reading

Anderson, Norman, and Brown, Walter. *Halley's Comet.* New York: Dodd, Mead, 1981.
Prepares the reader for the return of the most famous comet of all. This book also describes comets in general and gives tips on how readers can search for new comets. (Intermediate)

Asimov, Isaac. *How Did We Find Out About: Comets?* New York: Walker, 1975.
Tells of the discovery of comets and of the fascinating histories of the better known ones, such as Halley's, Encke's, and Biela's. (Beginner)

Ciaccio, Edward. "Celestial Debris." *Astronomy,* May 1983, pp. 6-22.
Discusses in detail the latest theories about comets, asteroids, and meteorites, and the ways in which these objects may be linked. (Advanced)

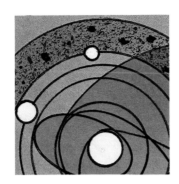

 **Index**

Andromedids, 35
asteroid belt, 39
asteroids: Apollo objects,
    43-44; Ceres, 39; C-type,
    40; Deimos, 43; Hermes,
    13; Hygeia, 39; M-type, 40;
    original, 40-42; Pallas, 39;
    Phobos, 43; S-type, 39-40;
    Trojan, 42; Vesta, 39;
    Victoria, 43; 1976 UA, 13;
    1983 TB, 44
astroblemes, 48

Barringer crater, 14, 48
Biela's comet, 28-29, 33-34
Bieliid meteor storm, 34

Chiron, 44-45
coma, of comet, 21
comets: long-period, 23-27;
    orbits of, 20-25; parts of,
19-23; short-period,
    23-27; sun-grazers, 26-27;
    Tunguska event and, 13,
    48-49
constellation, 35
core, of comet, 19

Deimos, 17
diameter, 15

Encke's comet, 27-28

Ganymede, 17
Geminid meteor shower, 44
gravity, 15

Halley's comet, 25-26, 52
Hermes, 13

Jupiter family, 25

Leonids, 35-37

meteorites: chondrites, 50;
     impact craters of, 13-14,
     47-48; irons, 49-50;
     origins of, 50-51; size of,
     47; stones, 49-50;
     stony-irons, 49-50
meteoroid, 32-33
meteors, 14, 31-32, 34-37
meteor showers, 34-37, 44
meteor storm, 34, 37
micrometeoroids, 32
moons, 15-17

Neptune family, 25
nucleus, of comet, 19

Oort Cloud, 24, 45
orbits, 15-17, 20-25

Perseids, 35-37
planets, 15

satellites, 15-17
shooting stars, 14, 31
solar system, 15-17
solar wind, 21
Swift-Tuttle comet, 35

tail, of comet, 21-22
Taurids, 35
Temple-Tuttle comet, 35
Tunguska event, 13, 48-49

1976 UA, 13

Vredefort Ring, 48

zodiacal cloud, 32-33